Happy 21st Birthday

*Happy 21st Birthday*

# A Field Guide for
# Bar Patrons of All Ages

## Tanya P. Frantzen

ISBN-13: 978-0-692-15521-9 (Softcover)

ISBN-10: 0-692-15521-X (Softcover)

Front cover design and interior artwork by **Violet Aveline**

Book design by **Dale A. Nibbe**

First Edition

Author contact information:
happy21stbirthdaybook@gmail.com

Available from Amazon.com and other retail outlets

# Contents

# Dedication

This book is dedicated to the amazing people I have had the pleasure of working with throughout the years, especially the staff at the B-Side and the Basement Pub. Y'all are the greatest.

Asla—
I love you!
More than you
know! This book
is funny as FUCK!!!...
And I hope that you'll
~~like~~ it...

Dear Reader

Love You, Jazzy

There is a reason I wrote this book. And there is a reason you are holding it in your hand.

1) You are smart enough to understand that you don't know everything you need to know about bars. You have taken a step to educate yourself on the etiquette of dive bar culture.

That's great. Self-education is never a bad thing. I sincerely hope my experience can help you learn what you need to know.

2) Someone in your life got it for you as a gift. That person is AWESOME. They have had good times in bars and would like you to do the same. Also, they want to keep you out of trouble.

You can go ahead and send them a thank-you card from your bartender.

3) You are a bartender yourself. We bartenders know that only other bartenders really understand what it is we do for a living. We love to swap stories about the things we see and the assholes we encounter and discuss the finer points of our profession.

4) You would like to become a bartender. If you read this whole book and still want to follow that career path, you will be well armed, and one step ahead of the game.

I have worked twenty-five years in the service industry, twenty of those years in dive bars. I think I have a pretty good handle on them.

I wrote this guide as an attempt to share some of that experience with you.

What I hope to accomplish is this:

- I want you, dear reader, to become my favorite customer. And I, and those like me, your favorite bartender.
- I want you to laugh. At yourself, and at others.
- I want you to learn the difference between bad service on the part of the bartender and miscommunication. Between bad service and bad timing. Between bad service and just being in the wrong bar. And the difference between the bartender being an asshole and you being an asshole.
- I want you to be able to expect that your bartenders treat you with respect and provide service that earns your repeat business, as well as your tips. I want you to be able to recognize excellent service.
- I want to share with potential bartenders what they need to know to be awesome at their jobs.
- I want you bartenders to know you are not alone. I feel your pain, buddy.

There is an abundance of blogs, Facebook pages, zines, books, and magazines that are dedicated to bitching about the customer.

This is not one of them.

Everything I read from bartenders is a rant about how customers are jerks and don't tip. "Top 10 Ways to Get on Your Bartender's Bad Side," "Your Bartender Hates You," or even "25

Ways to Guarantee Your Bartender Will Spit in Your Drink."

There are a lot of "do this, don't do that" snarky instructions written in a huff after a long, especially trying shift at the pub. They masquerade as lessons but are really just rants.

I understand the need for them. When people get off work, they need to vent a bit, and bartenders are no exception. Most people just go down to the bar for a couple before going home. We bartenders don't have that luxury, so ranting on the internet it is.

But . . .

These lists and rants further the notion that bartenders are just jerks and yet you are expected to tip them for the pleasure of receiving their bad attitude. "The customer is always wrong." "Customers are THE WORST!"

I'm here to say that's not how we really feel.

Also, we are professionals who would NEVER spit in somebody's drink, no matter how rude they are. (If someone is so painful to deal with that we feel like spitting in their drink, we just cut them off or send them home. We have that power!) Just so you know. We really don't do that.

Maybe you can tell by now, I am not one of those bartenders who think the customer is always wrong. I believe that most of the time when a customer is frustrating to the bartender (and vise versa), it is because they just don't know any better—on *both* sides. I will attempt to open the conversation. To create understanding between the server and the served. To educate servers and customers alike on the issues that create problems in that relationship.

THERE ARE A LOT OF TERRIBLE SERVERS IN THIS BUSINESS.

On the other hand, THERE ARE A LOT OF TERRIBLE CUSTOMERS TOO.

I do at points in this book get a little ranty about the shitty things people do and say to me while I'm working. I do this to make points. To show you what NOT to do or how to approach things in a way that won't end with the bartender posting about you on their *Bartender Rant* blog. Or kicking you out. Or serving you short shots. Or whatever. I do it to give you a peek at what goes on in the bartender's mind. Insight into why the things bartenders complain about are so frustrating to us. A view from behind the ice well.

I want you to have a head start to being the awesomest customer ever . . . therefore having the most fun, receiving the most free drinks, having insider status, and being invited to the most after-hours parties at your favorite watering hole.

Bartenders, there are lessons in here for you too.

Being a bartender is easy. Just ask anyone who slung drinks for a summer in college.

Being an excellent bartender, however, is a whole different story.

This story.

Here you go. I wrote it all down for you.

Now . . . can I get you a drink?

Tanya

# 1

## Introduction

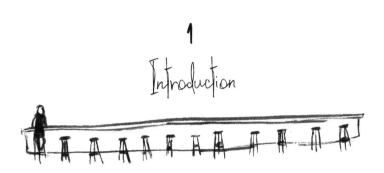

I live in Portland, Oregon. Every year it rains from Halloween to Independence Day. To save you some calculations, that's from October to July. Nine months. Let that sink in for a minute. There may be ten days total when one can actually get a glimpse of the sun during the whole nine months.[1]

We take our entertainments quite seriously here. Portland is a city that has more microbreweries, strip clubs, and state parks per capita than any other city in the US. Our coffee is organic, free trade, delicious, and roasted up the street. Our strip clubs are full nude with alcohol (a combination I understand is difficult to find elsewhere, even in Vegas). In the summer we have theater troupes who perform full episodes of *Star Trek* in the park. We have the Adult Soapbox Derby (alcohol plus gravity! what could be more fun?), well-loved roller derby teams, insane

---

1 But spring is beautiful. When the sun shines for the first time in months, you can literally see things growing before your eyes. Everyone gets on a bicycle and rides it to WHEREVER. People will just stand on the sidewalk facing the sun and sighing. It's amazing.

soccer fans, circus troupes, amazing drum corps that show up at events and make the most simple evening epic, a thriving music scene, theater, comics, film, art (lots of art), twenty-one-and-over video game arcades, and more James Beard Award–winning chefs than you can shake a foie gras profiterole at.

AND BARS. SO MANY BARS.

I firmly believe that this is how we avoid an epidemic of suicide every May and June. We haven't seen the sun in so long we can barely get out of bed. So, in the interest of survival . . .

We go to rock shows. We make art. We have BBQs where you bring something to grill, a tarp, any pulleys you have, and rope. (The yard ends up looking like a homeless encampment, but hey, at least we're outside. And sorta dry.) We see movies in theaters that sell alcohol. But mostly, we go to the neighborhood tavern and commiserate with our fellow wet, sun-deprived Portlanders. We get drunk together.

The Portland dive bar scene is, in my humble, unbiased opinion, the best anywhere. We need it for survival; therefore, we cherish it. The bar is our escape, our respite from the constant drizzle and gray sky. It is also our living room and where we find our family.

These places are where I have spent my twenties and thirties. I have worked in them, patronized them, spent Christmases and Thanksgivings in them.

Eventually I opened one of my own. It's my favorite place.

Most of what I know and think about bars I learned in these places. Twenty years.

Maybe you will disagree with my opinions. I have a lot to say on the subject, and some of it may get you shaking your head.

Go ahead. Write me a letter telling me all about it. Or better yet, write your own book. Call it *Why Tanya's Wrong*.

I can't wait to read it.

# 2

## That's a Big Word for a Bartender

There are noble, brave professions in this world. Nurses, teachers, cops, doctors, firefighters. These people put their lives at risk every day to make the world a better place and serve their community.

Bartending isn't one of them. It is an important community service nonetheless.

Jobs where the difference between life and death can depend on someone's skill and ability to think quickly are stressful and super taxing. Burnout is a serious concern.

On a day off, those with important jobs need to relax. Unwind. They need a little downtime, a couple of drinks, a chance to let off some steam.

The local tavern provides it for them. A safe place to unwind and wash off the stress.

I've been told that it's the only thing that makes it okay to go back to work, say, as a pediatric nurse. The shit they see. Abuse, neglect, really sick children. It wears on your soul. You need a recharge.

I sleep well at night. I provide a service to my community that I am proud of.

The neighborhood gathers under my watchful eye, and I make sure everyone has a good time and gets home safe. I am happy to do what I do for a living.

Don't get me wrong. I'm sure there are plenty of bartenders out there who are just biding time until their "real" career takes off. Just ask 99 percent of the actors in LA.

My colleagues and I are not them. We are professional bartenders and love doing it.

"Professional bartender" is usually said in reference to the cocktail wizards, or mixologists. Those guys make excellent drinks and are really good at their jobs.

What people forget is that us ladies at the corner dives are also professionals. We are also very good at our jobs. It's just that our jobs are different than theirs. Also, we don't wear bow ties.

This misunderstanding becomes clear to me when I hear someone say (which I heard quite often before I became The Owner), "You know what? I see how much money you make in a six-hour shift, for doing a pretty easy, fun job. I think I will just quit my HR/marketing/graphic design job and bartend for a summer. I could save a ton of money!"

Okay. I understand what you are talking about. I do love my job. It is an awesome job. I am trusted by the owner to run the show by myself. I make $100 to $300 a night in tips (on a day shift, I'm lucky if I break a hundy), plus the meager paycheck I get each month, which is less than $300 for a whole month, as I am taxed heavily on tips. I don't have to split my tips with anyone, because I am doing seven jobs myself. Bartender, cook, janitor, prep cook, security/door person, barback, cocktail waitress. All me. And I can actually do all those jobs at once because I have done each of them at one time or another and have the experience it takes to multitask them all.

But what you don't understand is that this job is not available to you. You have zero experience bartending and no desire to work at a bar for more than a summer. This job is available to me because of my fifteen years' experience in the service industry, and because I plan on working at this bar for a long time.

The kind of job you can get for the summer is nothing like my awesome job.

A summer bartending job for someone with no experience is either at an old-man dive where you listen to the same story every day and serve cans of Busch Light to retired old drunks. You will make $15 to $50 during each ten-hour shift. Or you could get a summer job at a club of some sort, but there you will work with six to eight other people—cooks, barbacks, security guards, cocktail waitresses, and so on. The $300 tip pool has to be split about eight different ways. You end up with $50 a night, if you're lucky. Even at a club, corporate bar, or resort, you have to start at the bottom. It could take three years for you to work your way up to bartending.

My problem with this "I will just bartend for a summer" statement is that you are implying that the job I do is easy to do, and easy to get. Anyone can do it.

While this may be true for some bartending jobs, mine is not one of them. I have worked hard to get here. It took fifteen years in the service industry before I was able to get this awesome, autonomous, lucrative, and fun job.

If you are serious about wanting to work for a summer in a place like this, here's how you do it.

Get a job as a busser in a chain restaurant. Move up to waiter, then barback, and eventually bartender.

After these three years at Chili's, Red Robin, Old Chicago, or Applebee's, you can try to get a bartending job in an independently owned tavern. Slowly, with a lot of networking, you can move up in the bartending world, getting better and better jobs every couple of years. Then, maybe, with some skill and hard work, you will eventually end up in a place like this, with a job like mine.

So please, Mr. HR/Marketing/Graphic Design, go ahead and get a summer bartender gig. Give me a call in ten years and let me know where you are working. I will come by and tip you a few dollars.

"Just a bartender."

It's true. I've heard it said. To my face.

People assume that because I am a bartender, I have somehow failed at becoming what I really wanted to be or that I am so totally unskilled that it's the only job I can get.

They think I am trying to get a real job, a real career, and my bar job is just what I am doing until I succeed at what I really want to do with my life. Or that I'm bummed that I "ended up" tending bar.

Here's a clue . . .

I LOVE MY JOB.

I CHOSE MY JOB.

I sleep well at night knowing I provide a much-needed service to my community. And I am really good at it.

# 3
## Finding Your Bar

A bar is not a bar is not a bar.

Dive bars, gay bars, tiki bars, martini bars, corporate bars, hotel bars, dance clubs, airport bars, karaoke bars, wine bars, and strip clubs.

So many different types of watering holes. And they all have differing experiences to offer.

A lot of things that go wrong in bars go wrong because the bar you're in is not the bar you are looking for or the bar you think it is.

So please, when you go to a bar for the first time, LOOK AROUND.

Is there table service? A visible menu? Silverware? Martini glasses? A customer order station? A waitress station? A bouncer? One bartender or three? A smoking patio? A stage?

One bad Yelp review that my bar has gotten goes a little like this: "My friends seem to like this place, but I don't understand it. I waited for 20 minutes for a server to come over, and when he finally did, it took another 10 to get my drink. He didn't even drop off a menu. I don't recommend ordering a Gibson. Mine was terrible. Meh. 2 stars."

Let me tell you about that for a minute.

In case you didn't know, a Gibson is a martini with a cocktail onion instead of an olive (more on that in chapter 9).

My bar is a neighborhood dive tavern. One bartender, an order well, and no martini glasses. We *can* make martinis but don't do them very often. We put them in a highball glass (what we call a "bucket").

Of course your Gibson was terrible. That cocktail onion HAS BEEN THERE SINCE 1997.

Of course he didn't drop off a menu.

THERE IS NO MENU.

Of course you waited twenty minutes for the server to come over.

THERE. IS. NO. SERVER.

What I imagine happened that night, because I've seen it over and over again, is something like this . . .

She came in and sat down at a table.

The bartender was busy, a line at the bar eight deep. Dishes piling up.

The bartender saw her sit down and gave her a minute to figure it out. When she didn't, he came over to (a) welcome her and say hi, (b) check her ID, and (c) let her know that the way it works here is customers come up to the bar to get their drinks.

But instead, when he arrived at her table, she said, "Gibson," when he started to say, "Hi."

Now, the bartender has a choice.

Spend a few minutes (a) getting over how rude she is and (b) explaining to her how it works (which, when dealing with someone who's oblivious, takes a little time). He also knows there's way too much to do. If he spends too much time talking to her, that's time added to the wait for the customers who are doing it right, in line at the well.

Or, he can just go make her a Gibson, after serving the people at the bar, and bring it over to her. (Takes ten minutes. And the people in line don't have to wait as long.)

So, he chose right.

At this point he doesn't care if her Gibson is terrible or if she has to wait.

Judging from her rudeness and lack of awareness of her surroundings, he figures (correctly, as evidenced by the Yelp review) she won't come back, no matter what he does. She already hates her experience and is having a bad time. Also, she won't tip anyway, and nothing he can do will change her mind. He has been given no chance to earn her repeat business and her tip, other than dropping his other duties and ignoring every other person in the bar.

He doesn't really want her back anyway.

If this girl had come in, looked, seen the line with a big sign over it that says ORDER HERE, she would have noticed a few things. There is no drink menu. There is no rack of martini glasses. There is no vermouth on display (which is required to make a Gibson). There is no cocktail server.

There IS a lot of whiskey and local microbrews.

The conversation could have gone like this:

"Gibson, please!"

"Well, we can make Gibsons, but we're not really set up for martinis here. And they're not that great. How about a gin and tonic? Or, if you'd like, I make a pretty good margarita."

"Okay. Sure. Thanks."

At which point, the bartender, if he gets a good vibe off her, could upgrade her liquor to something more delicious than the cheap well booze. At no extra charge. Or even just get her first drink on the house. Just because he feels bad that he can't make the drink she really wants or make it well, given the tools at his disposal. He wants her to enjoy her cocktail. He wants her to come back. He wants to provide good service.

Awesome Yelp review in 3 . . . 2 . . . 1 . . .

If what you want is a well-made martini and table service, you really should go to a place with tablecloths.

The neighborhood dive full of bike messengers that is blasting death metal is, generally, not going to suit your needs.

This seems like common sense to me. But in all my years behind bars I have come to learn that it's true what they say.

Common sense is, indeed, not all that common.

Cocktail bars are awesome. They have professional mixologists (I hate this word) on staff and have put research, thought, skill, and hours of tasting experimental cocktail recipes into making their drink menu.

And those drinks are delicious.

Cocktail bartenders can be expected to know how, and have the necessary tools, to make most cocktails. If they don't know how to make the drink you want, they have the resources to find out. That sort of bartending is more like chemistry or food science than what I have been doing for twenty years. I, personally, am not that great at it.

Okay. Let's be honest. I'm terrible at it.

What those drinks are NOT, however, is cheap.

The payroll at a fancy cocktail bar has to be about seven times that of a regular neighborhood dive. My payroll, and the taxes that go with it, costs me about $4,000 a month. I have only one person working at all times except for a barback for a couple of hours on Friday and Saturday nights. To make fancy cocktails in a timely manner, serve them in expensive martini glasses, and offer food to accompany them takes no less than two bartenders, one barback, two cooks, a dishwasher, and a door guy. That's seven times the staff. That's seven times the payroll. Minimum.

That's why the martini costs $14.

One random busy night at the bar, a customer said to me, "Wow, your drinks are so cheap! I love it!" Not one minute later she said, "Man, you really should hire another person to help. The line is pretty long."

Well . . . which is it, lady?

I could hire someone to help, have two bartenders on at all times, but there go the cheap drinks. That extra $4,000 a month has to come from somewhere.

Some dive bars offer food and perhaps a few fancy cocktails. But remember this: Expect that your fancy cocktail be made with a few shortcuts. Expect your food to take a long time and not be made fresh to order. That's why your martini is $5 instead of $15. It's not going to be delicious.

I guess my point is, you gotta pick one or the other. Cheap drinks or fancy ones. Cheap drinks or good food. Cheap drinks or table service.

Sorry to burst this particular bubble, but you really can't have it all.

# 4

## On Being a Regular

The regular watering hole has the potential to become your extended family. The power of community and shared experience should not be underestimated.

At my bar, on any given day, there will be a doctor, an auto mechanic, a building inspector, a carpenter and his electrician buddy, two dishwashers, three nurses, an arborist studying to become a politician, ex-military, current military, a county judge, two mechanical engineers, a comic book artist, lawyers, and independent movie producers. Social workers, hackers, lighting techs, community developers, a ballet dancer, a historian, and an amateur aerialist. Not to mention all the chefs, bartenders, and musicians. SO MANY MUSICIANS.

If I wanted to take over the world, I would have all the help I could possibly need, for the price of a round for the house.

Every single one of these people will help each other move. Come over for a BBQ and, while there, rewire the electrical panel. Or dog-sit. Or babysit. Resurface the deck, defrag the computer, read and critique the book draft. (Shout-out . . . !)

Their band will play your party. They will send out a nice bottle of wine "compliments of the kitchen" while you are out on a date or trying to impress the in-laws. (These gestures should be met in kind, or at the very least, buy that chef buddy a drink next time you see them.)

They will keep their ears open for a new job for you or introduce you to someone who can help. Trade their truck for your car when you need to pick up a couch. Put you on the guest list for the sold-out show. Theater tickets, loaner tools. They will stop you from driving home when you've had one too many and let you sleep it off on their couch.

They will leave you alone when you need solitude, buy you a drink when you're broke, and listen when you need an ear. Walk you home when there's sketchy stuff going on in the neighborhood. Loan you money, and pay you back the money they borrowed.

In short, bar communities are awesome.

With all this greatness comes a little responsibility. It's not too hard and takes minimal effort. But it is really important.

You are responsible for setting the tone of the room. Acting the way we want everyone else to act.

You, as a regular, will be held to a standard of behavior, as part of a carefully constructed atmosphere. Your transgressions are more easily forgiven if you are a regular, especially if you are the one who offers to fix the broken whatever or brings all of the empties from your table with you when you come to the bar.

We don't care that you were drunk yesterday, who you're sleeping with, or that you were broke that one time and didn't tip.

We cut you a bit of slack, but we expect you to lead by example.

If a dude who's never been in before sees you make an inappropriate joke or teasingly slap the bartender's ass and not get immediately kicked out, that new guy will forever believe that slapping the bartender's ass is acceptable behavior in this establishment. Yeah, we are close, you, Mr. Regular, and I. We joke like that a lot, when I am not working. I know you were just kidding, and no harm really comes from your actions. The creepy dude at the end of the bar, however, doesn't know. I will blame you, forever, if that guy touches me just once.

It's okay to feel a little superiority toward newcomers. You were there first, after all, and the fact that they discovered your gem of a local dive changes it for you a little. But remember, an influx of new faces is absolutely necessary to the survival of the business. It doesn't change your favorite place as drastically as if it were to go under (which is what happens to bars that become exclusive insider clubs). Be nice to them. Don't stop and stare when they walk through the door for the first time. Let them join in your conversation at the bar, and please don't make fun of them out loud. If they turn out to be assholes, don't worry. They will figure out they're in the wrong place soon enough.

Just give them a chance. You were new once too.

Another responsibility that comes with "regular" status is you are the eyes and ears of the bartender. You are responsible for letting them know what's happening that they can't see.

No toilet paper in the bathroom?

I can't count how many times I have closed the bar after a busy night and found the paper dispenser empty and the toilet clogged with paper towels. WHAT??? How long has it been like that? WHY DIDN'T ANYONE TELL ME???

I understand not wanting to be the bearer of bad news. You don't want to bother the bartender while they're working. But what most people don't understand is how grateful we are to those who point it out to us. I was so busy I never had a chance to check it myself and just assumed everything was okay. I take pride in providing good service, which includes toilet paper. I gotta know if something needs my attention.

Most times I am so grateful I will buy you a drink. Or two if you ask for the keys to go change it out for me.

Someone's about to get into a fight, doing coke in the bathroom for an hour, loudly declaring racist bullshit, relentlessly hitting on women who want to be left alone, or generally making people uncomfortable?

Usually these problems are obvious to the bartender. We watch for that stuff as a matter of habit, but sometimes we miss it. Please let the bartender know if you see a problem forming. It helps the bartender prepare for the confrontation or, better yet, helps everyone avoid a scene altogether.

Burnt-out light bulbs. Broken glass. Wasted assholes. Flat soda.

We expect our regulars to let us know about these things, but the flat soda is one I really depend on regulars for. I am pouring whiskey sodas all night but have not tasted one. If the canister is bad or the $CO_2$ is low, the drinks I am serving taste like crap, losing me customers and tips.

If someone would tell me, "Hey, you should taste the soda. I think it's flat," it takes about one minute to change out the canister and replace all the flat drinks with new ones. "Hey there, turns out the soda is flat. How's your drink? Would you like to trade it in for a new one?"

When I do that, I have made a customer for life. I look awesome and have provided great, above-and-beyond service. I am grateful to you for bringing it to my attention. Thank you, my lovely assistant. Your next drink's on me.

A regular will be the person who keeps the bartender company on slow days. You will become buddies, if not friends. This is awesome. We love that you are there to chat with when there's nothing else that we have to do.

But when it's busy, please don't start a long story when I'm in the weeds. I will be forced to walk away in the middle.

If there's a line at the bar six deep and I am running my ass off, this IS NOT THE TIME to ask me about how the new band is going or to show me new pictures of your dog. Paying attention to the small talk (or worse, the big talk) is totally throwing me off my game. The best I can do for you is nod and say, "Mm-hmm." It sucks, because I do love talking to you. Just not right now.

As I mentioned, working at dive bars means you wear many hats. It seems like serving drinks is the whole job, but it really is a small part of what the bartender is responsible for. It happens often that I have a line at the well and have to power through to make sure everyone gets their drinks without a wait. While I take care of this, dishes are piling up, food orders are waiting, the outside area needs bussing, and the ashtrays need emptying. I hear there's no paper towels in the men's room. There's a disturbance in the corner that might possibly turn into a fight, and a glass was broken at one of the outside tables. Plus my bladder is FULL. I am speed-bartending the line through, because I don't want my thirsty people to have to wait too long, and then I have a list of things needing my attention. Invariably, as soon as the line is down, a regular sitting at the bar will start talking to me about whatever is on their mind. "Great! Now that you have a minute, I have a question for you!"

I'm sorry. I don't actually have a minute. I have a bunch of things to do, and I have to go do them before a new line forms. I'm sure it feels like I am ignoring you or am uninterested in talking to you. Please don't take it personally. If I stop to chat, the line will be back in no time. Also, I have had to pee for two hours, and if I don't go now, I won't have a chance for at least another hour.

If I have time to chat, I will come over and say hey. If I don't do that, please assume I have a to-do list in my head and leave me to it.

If you say, "I have a question for you when you got a minute," I promise you have made it onto the mental list, and I will get to you as soon as I am done with all the other stuff on that list. Sorry.

Again, having a small staff means cheap drinks in a cozy atmosphere but also often means no time to chat.

An example of how awesome a regular crowd can be? Sure! Here ya go.

Door slammed open, and a random guy stormed in.

"Is this another fucking gay bar???!!! Every bar in this town I go to turns out to be a fucking gay bar!!!!"

The room fell silent. We all just stared at this asshole, blank-faced and shocked.

I looked around and noticed some people had started to nod apologetically. Inspired, and grateful for the wit and unity of my regulars, I said, "Sorry, buddy. Try up the street. There might not be any gays there."

Now, the bar isn't actually a "gay bar." It's a neighborhood bar. There happen to be some gays in the neighborhood, a good number of whom patronize the establishment.

We, collectively and without discussion, decided none of us wanted to hang out with that dude and hoped he would go someplace else.

If anyone had said, "No, this isn't a gay bar," we would have had that guy among us. At least long enough to convince him to go somewhere else. No thank you.

That day I bought a round for the house.

# 5

## On Dating Bartenders

So, you have a crush on your bartender?
No shit, stupid.

She is doing her job. Well. That job is to make you feel good for having patronized the establishment where she works.

This job, in regard to you, entails the following:

- She smiles at you every time you walk through her door. She's really glad you came in tonight.
- She listens carefully to what you want and does her very best to provide it for you just the way you like it.
- She thinks you're funny. Hilarious, even. You haven't told a single joke yet that has failed to make her laugh.
- She calmly pays attention to whatever is on your mind. She cares about how your day went, gives you advice on dealing with your boss, gives you leads on a new job, and so on. She pays such good attention she even knows how you want her to react. Listen? Commiserate? Change the subject? Buy you a shot? Leave you alone? Tell you a funny story? Introduce you to someone who loves talking

about the stuff you love talking about? Run you a tab until tomorrow? She's got it covered.

- She totally ignores your faults. She doesn't nag about how you spend your money, how you dress, or how late you come home. And never about how much you drink.
- She dresses up so she can look nice whenever you see her.
- The more time you spend with her, the better you feel. Each short conversation ends with her handing you a glass of alcohol. After a few of these conversations, you will forget that you are getting drunk and only remember that she smiled at you and made you feel better.
- She covers for you. She has your back. She spends her time watching over you and making sure everything is okay for you.
- She lets you get away with slightly inappropriate flirting but gently puts you in line too.

All this she does with compassion, attention to your needs, and a smile.

Without judgment.

She sounds like the PERFECT GIRLFRIEND, right? Of course you think you are in love with her. And maybe you are.

However, it's more likely that she is just really awesome at her job.

If you have taken this into account and still think there is a chance she might actually be interested, there is a way to go about asking her out. It's pretty hard to pull off and has very little chance of success, but it's the best chance you'll get.

Just remember, if she is open to dating you, she has probably dated the guy on the bar stool next to you.

Here goes . . .

The most important thing is this: DO NOT ORDER A DRINK.

If she is serving you, you are a customer. Her job is to try to say yes to you in all situations that aren't inappropriate. She will have to choose between saying yes to you on the spot or putting you in the "inappropriate" category. In all my years behind the bar, I never once said yes. Just the fact that the guy asking me out was willing to put me in that situation was enough for me to decide I didn't want to date him. He obviously isn't very thoughtful or just doesn't care enough to try to avoid putting me in an uncomfortable spot.

"Sorry. I don't date customers. Thanks, though!" Smile, offer a drink, and be done with that dude.

She could say maybe, but that's because she doesn't want to hurt your feelings or make you uncomfortable. She is at work, and her job is to make you feel good.

DO NOT FIND HER ON SOCIAL MEDIA.

This is a place for her and her friends. It may be your goal to be there someday, but you're not there yet. It's quite possibly her personal space that she keeps separate from her bartender persona.

Find a time when you know it will be slow at the bar while she is working. Afternoon maybe?

"No, thanks. I'm not here to drink today. But I'd like to talk to you if you have a free minute."

And wait. Patiently. Have something to do. A newspaper, some homework maybe. Keep yourself occupied but available. And away from other customers.

Being out of earshot is real important. She has to appear in control, and the other customers have to respect her. She can't say yes. She also has to appear attainable and kind. She can't say no. It seems like it shouldn't be that big of a deal. But again, putting her in that position doesn't help your case at all.

Once you have her attention, try this: "I like you. You're really good at your job. I enjoy talking to you and would like the chance to get to know you outside of your professional capacity as my bartender. Maybe I can make you a drink sometime. Or dinner. Or coffee. Your choice. If you'd like that, please give me a call."

Make sure you write your name legibly. She could only know you as "whiskey ginger with a lime, nice guy, always wears hats."

End of conversation. Leave. Do not stay for a drink.

I repeat: LEAVE.

The leaving is important because it shows her these things about you:

- You really were just there to ask her out. Not as a customer.
- You have a life outside of going to the bar. You got shit to do.
- You are unwilling to put her in the position of accepting or rejecting you while she is working. It shows you have respect for her as a professional.

She can think about it and decide in her own time.

The next day, or maybe the day after, you should resume your regular bartender-customer relationship. Don't come in more or less often. Don't tip more or less than normal. And for the love of God, do not pester her about getting back to you. She hasn't forgotten.

Your confidence in this, in keeping everything cool and not being weird about it, may well be the deciding factor for her.

If she brings it up, "Sorry I haven't called . . . ," feel free to remind her that she should keep your number in case she's free sometime, but for now, "I'll have a whiskey ginger with a lime, please."

This shows that you are fine with keeping your customer relationship as is and are not the kind of guy who will make a girl's work uncomfortable if she doesn't want to date you. It may even make her want to date you.

Good luck.

Afterthought: I only know what I know. And that happens to be a female bartender's point of view. And just one person's point of view at that.

I really don't speak for all women bartenders. And very few men. But there it is. That's what I think. (See intro, *Why Tanya's Wrong.*)

# 6
## On Being Wasted in Public

I'm not an idiot.

Opinionated, somewhat scatterbrained, sure. But not stupid.

I know you have figured out by now how to get drunk. What I am trying to impart to you is how to be drunk in public and still be welcome in bars.

First things first.

IT'S OKAY TO BE DRUNK.

Wait, WHAT?? (said every bartender who just read that)

Just take a deep breath and let me explain.

We bartenders make a fairly decent, mostly enjoyable living getting people drunk. How dare we be pissed when someone gets drunk? It's part of our job to get them there.

Being drunk is not a problem. Being a drunk asshole, however, is.

People go out to bars for a million different reasons and have different expectations of the experience they are looking for.

One indisputable fact: When drinking is involved, people will end up drunk. Pretty much the end of the story on that.

The bartender's job is to make sure that you, and everyone else in the room, have a good time doing just that. Getting drunk.

Drinks will be spilled.

Glasses will be broken.

People will not get along with each other.

Clothes will come off.

There will be vomit.

There will be graffiti.

There will be bathroom sex.

And generally, bad decisions will be made.

It's how you handle it that determines your standing in the bar.

Sometimes things happen. For example, glasses get broken. This is okay. To all of the people who accidentally break a glass or knock into a table or trip on something and assume they will get kicked out, this is not necessarily the case. Don't freak out. It does happen a lot, and to people who aren't drunk. I won't send you home for having bad luck or being clumsy. I will, however, send you home for being visibly intoxicated. Don't worry, I can tell the difference.

Please don't yell at me, "I'm gonna get 86'd and I'm not even drunk! Bartenders are such power-hungry assholes!"

Well, I *was* going to just clean up the glass and get you a replacement drink, because I know that you aren't drunk. The tables wobble, and shit happens. I actually felt bad that happened to you. But if you assume I am a power-hungry asshole and am going to kick you out, and therefore yell at me, you can go right ahead and leave.

When your bartender looks at you and shakes her head, pay attention. That means you're about to do something that will put you firmly on her bad side. You really don't want to be there.

If she suggests a smaller beer, or one with lower ABV, or that you skip the shot this round, or maybe it's time to call it a night . . .

LISTEN TO HER!

She knows better than you how drunk you are. Or how drunk you will be when those last two shots finally hit your system.

You are not in trouble. She's not mad at you. She doesn't think you are a jerk or unable to hold your liquor.

SHE REALLY IS ON YOUR SIDE.

She wants you to have a good time, which she knows won't happen when you start acting the fool. She's trying to protect you from making an ass of yourself.

So she stops you before you do something stupid.

Bartender: Hey, maybe it's time to call it a night. I'm cutting you off. You've been here for seven hours and had fourteen drinks . . . I'd feel better if we could talk tomorrow . . .

Customer: WHY AM I BEING 86'D??? WHAT DID I DO???? FUCK THIS PLACE!!! ARE YOU A RACIST? ARE YOU A HOMOPHOBE? WHY DO YOU HATE ME? I DIDN'T DO ANYTHING!!!!

Okay, drama queen, chill the fuck out. You didn't do anything wrong. It's just that the liver can only process one drink an hour, and you've had two every hour for the past seven hours and haven't eaten anything. You're about to become a problem. If I send you home right now, I won't actually have to 86 you when the liquor hits your system.

Sidenote: There's a big difference between *cut off* and *86'd*.

To be 86'd means you are never allowed back through the door. 86'd is what assholes get. 86'd means the bartender will never ever serve you again. You've messed up so bad, and so repeatedly, that it's not even worth the conversation to decide if you should be allowed back in.

*Cut off* means no more alcohol for you tonight, but you are totally welcome to come back tomorrow. Even stay tonight, but only if you aren't drinking any more.

It's also possible that the bartender knows something you don't.

Maybe she can smell the weed in your pocket and knows

the cops are about to show up for something totally unrelated. She doesn't want your obvious smell of an illegal substance in the room when they get there, you know, because of your outstanding warrant. Maybe your ex is on his way and the bartender knows you become a mess when you see him.

Maybe you're about to get into a fight and don't know it.

But most likely, she just knows your limits and you're about to exceed them.

Depending on your past behavior and the trust the bartender has in you, there may be room for negotiation.

"Oh . . . okay. Maybe I don't need another strong microbrew and a huge shot of whiskey. How about just a small draft beer and some chips or peanuts or something? Then I will go home."

Food. Yes. ANY FOOD. There's a valve in your stomach that is open when your stomach has only liquid in it but closes for solid food. This slows the absorption of alcohol into your blood system. Every bartender knows this, and if you eat, they may just serve you one more.

The bartender isn't stupid. He knows what you're up to. He is a professional host to a party of strangers every single night. If you are out to get wasted, he will help you do that right up until you become a liability. Then he will try to stop you. If "getting wasted" is a common thing for you, or the whole reason you are in the bar in the first place, having mutual respect, trust, and good tipping etiquette will go a long way to accomplishing that goal. Leaving when asked will allow the bartender to trust you, and he will give you more and more leniency as time goes on. On the other hand, if trying to send you home went badly for him, he will forever cut you off before he has to. He has plenty of shit to do and doesn't have the time to fight with you about it. So if arguing is your thing, he will have the conversation with you while you are still relatively sober, if only to spare himself the hassle.

If you smile, tip, and say, "Yeah. I came out tonight to get drunk, and I guess I'm there. Thanks! Good job and you'll probably see me tomorrow for a hangover cure," he will trust you enough next time to serve you one more, despite his better judgment.

He will figure out your limits and hold you to them, but if he trusts you to behave semirationally (read: not argue with the bartender) even while drunk, he will let you get right up to that line.

# 1

## On Handling Problems

People get drunk. Fights happen.

As a bartender, it is my job to stop the fight from escalating. Or, if I am really on it, prevent it from starting in the first place.

The bartender's control over the room is paramount.

For everything to go well and everyone to have a good time, the bartender needs to be listened to and respected. There aren't many times that this becomes crucial, but when it is, it is everything.

It's the difference between a good night at the bar and talking to cops. It's the difference between a few tense words and a knife fight. It's the difference between funny stories and ambulance rides. It's the difference between your favorite bar still being open for business and your favorite bartender being in jail.

The best way to get a fight to end is to not let it start in the first place. If that fails, or it is too late, my best tactic is distraction.

When there's a Pissed-Off Dude, and suddenly my face is right in front of him, I can control him. If I am respected, seen as "friend," "booze provider," or even "Mom," I can calm him down.

I will have him. Eye contact, control, and respect. Authority.

He will listen to me when I suggest that he and I go outside to talk about it.

"Tell me what the other guy did to piss you off so bad. I have to know what to tell the police when they arrest him." Or, "I've been wanting to 86 that asshole for a year. I like you and hate him. Tell me what he did so I can kick him out, then we can go back inside." Or even, "Let's go smoke a joint."

(Please note that most of what I will say to that dude is total bullshit. Usually the one I have to manipulate into calming down is the one who's at fault. I will tell him anything I have to in order to get him to walk out the door. DON'T GET IN MY WAY, and whatever you do, don't contradict me. I'm lying to the guy.)

Once he is outside, I can simply shut the door behind him. Maybe lock it until he walks away.

Just getting him away from people looking at him is usually enough to get him to go away.

That scenario plays out all the time.

The only thing that will stop me from getting him to walk out the door is if someone takes that control away from me.

If you stand behind me, saying to Pissed-Off Dude (POD), "Yeah, you better listen to her!" What you're really saying is "You'd better do what I say." Even if what you are saying is "Do what she says," you've stolen the control out of my hands.

POD will break eye contact with me, point over my head at you, and say, "Come at me, bro!"

At that point I have lost it and there's nothing I can do to stop him from punching you.

You've taken control away from the one person in the room whom the POD might actually listen to.

You are responsible for the ensuing melee. Also, I will never again trust you to respect my authority in such matters.

The best thing you can do for your favorite bartender when he or she is dealing with an irate person is to ignore that person entirely but stay available. Close but unobtrusive, and out of the POD's line of sight. Maybe hang out near where the altercation is happening, if you can do so without drawing attention to yourself. Flip through the jukebox, pick up a magazine, pull out your phone and pretend to check your messages.

Near the door is a good place to stand, in case the bartender needs to push the dude out. Be ready to have that shit open.

Whatever you do, DO NOT GET IN THE MIDDLE. Do not threaten or try to involve your well-meaning self in any way. The more you act like you're not paying attention to him, the less POD will have to prove.

People don't pound their chests when nobody's watching.

There is one situation where you can step in. One situation only.

(Keep in mind I am a female bartender, and unskilled in any martial art. Unless the art of manipulating drunk assholes is considered "martial." Maybe it should be. I'd have a black belt five times over by now.)

That situation is as follows, and is only likely to happen if someone else is getting in the middle. The more people who try to get involved, the more likely POD will get violent.

Dude cocks back his arm in preparation to punch me in the face?

Fuck all that staying-out-of-the-way shit. Open season. Feel free to grab that guy by his eye sockets and toss him out the window.

Otherwise, stay out of my way. Dealing with assholes is my job, and I'm good at it, provided other drunk people don't try to help.

Another thing to keep in mind: Nobody gets served if I'm

filling out police reports. Or fixing broken chairs. Or calling ambulances.

All we want, those of us in the bar, is to go back to our drinks and talk about all the excitement. The only way we get to do that is if POD is gone.

The only person who has the authority to make that happen is me. If anyone else tries, they will likely get punched.

If not by Pissed-Off Dude, then maybe by me.

# 8
## On Tavern Ownership

Before you run out and buy a bar or rent a space to open a bar in, there are a few things you should do.

1) Go to your local neighborhood dive tavern. The one nearest to your house that still has carpet and three men over sixty sitting there before noon.

Go into the men's room and lie down on the floor. Reach around the toilet, and clasp your hands behind it.

Give it a good hug.

Stay there for one hour.

If you make it the whole hour, you may indeed have what it takes to run a bar.

If you're out in twenty minutes because you can't stand the smell and are about to lose your breakfast, you need to rethink your desire to be a bar owner. If you can't handle the questions posed to you by the old men trying to use the bathroom and convince them to either wait or use the ladies room just this one time, you need to look for a different career path. Tavern ownership just isn't for you.

2) Tend bar in at least three different situations: one with

terrible management, one with stellar management, and one with an extensive drink menu. Learn everything you can from your bosses and your coworkers. Why are the drinks priced that way? Why don't we carry this certain liquor? How much is your tax liability per year? What happens when there's a workers' comp claim or a liquor board violation?

3) Interview other bar owners. They should be proud of what they have accomplished, and provided you aren't planning to open up right next door and be the exact same kind of bar except with cheaper drinks, they will be more than happy to help you. Even if you are planning to open next door but are going for a different sort of clientele, they should want you to succeed. (Every time a bar opens up in our neighborhood, we get busier. More bars in the neighborhood = more drinkers in the neighborhood = great for everybody who serves drinks in the neighborhood. The fancy cocktail bar has runoff that we serve, as does the venue, the brewpub, and the arcade bar. If someone were to try to open a punk/metal dive bar with a heated smoking patio and a good local beer selection, however, I would wage war so fiercely I'd probably get arrested.)

4) Write a mission statement. Who is your clientele? What are your employees like? How expensive are your drinks? Food menu? Decor?

5) Take that mission statement and write out a business plan. This is so important I can't even stress it enough. Price out how much pint glasses cost—you will be buying at least a case a month. Ice machine maintenance, electric bill, payroll (how many staff hours per week?), art, jukebox, coolers, water bill, new toilet every six months or so, straws, napkins, limes, coffee. Workers' comp insurance, liquor liability insurance, slip-and-fall liability insurance, lawyer fees, debit card machine fees, ASCAP and BMI fees. (If you play music at the bar, ASCAP says you are making money off someone else's intellectual property. You have to pay for that or face steep fines.) Bank fees, "cash

deposited" fee. (That's true. If you deposit too much cash, the bank charges you. What. The. Fuck.) Permits (liquor license, alarm permit, health department permit, entertainment devices permit, lottery permit, sidewalk seating permit, etc.).

Chairs break. Coolers break. Ice machines break. Heating systems break. Tables need replacing, graffiti needs removing, walls need repainting. A lot of this you will do yourself, or you will pay others for their time to do it for you.

6) Look at all of the resources your local or state government has about getting and keeping a liquor license.

7) Talk to the neighborhood association about your location. Get them on your side. They actually have power with the local government, and if you piss them off, they can shut you down.

8) Give the devil a call and see if he is currently buying souls.

Let's talk about staffing for a second. Hiring well and treating your employees well is the key to success in the bar business. If you treat them as if they are stealing from you, they will steal from you. If you expect them to be lazy, they will be lazy.

The people running your place for you will be the face of your business. Your staffing choices will be the deciding factor of your success or failure. Unless all your best friends are professional bartenders with experience, work ethic, strong backbones, and personality, DON'T HIRE YOUR FRIENDS!

The worst kind of employee is the kind who thinks they're doing you a favor by standing behind your bar. Just ask my recently unemployed ex-friend.

Ever go into a bar and notice right away how obvious it is that the bartender hates his job?

Yeah?

Ever suggest that place to your friends?

Didn't think so.

Treat your employees like professionals, and they will be professionals. I pay my people above minimum wage, provide health insurance, and take them on vacations. Every single one of them is worth it. There is only one person working at a time, and they totally kill it every night. If I had lazy or entitled employees, I would need two at a time to run the bar. I would have to raise the prices and cut benefits in order to pay the extra payroll. Higher prices means fewer customers, which means fewer tips for the staff. Fewer tips means fewer happy employees, which means fewer customers. And the next thing you know, I'm looking for a job.

Some think I'm crazy for paying for health insurance. What they don't understand is that I can only afford it because the bar is so successful. It's successful because the staff is AWESOME. The staff is awesome because they love their jobs. I trust them and they trust me. They work really hard and look out for the interests of the company, and make great tips, pay, and benefits. I work really hard to keep them happy, and make profits.

It's a win-win.

Your bartenders know better than you do what's really going on in there. Trust them. If you don't trust them to make the right decisions, get rid of them and hire someone you can leave in charge and not worry.

## Customer Appreciation

There are many places in this book where I say, "I don't want those people in my bar." Or, "Maybe I will be spared their repeat business."

Most people think that any customer is a good customer. They're spending their money in your establishment, so you need to kiss their ass.

This is faulty reasoning.

If I have fifty people in the bar and five of them are annoying assholes, I am in danger of losing the other forty-five awesome people.

I have absolutely no hesitation about kicking the assholes the fuck out. I would rather have the good customers three times a week forever than those assholes' money just for today.

I don't like to hang out at bars where people are obnoxious, rude, or pissed off all the time, so why would my potential customers?

Getting rid of the shitty people may lose you their business, but the room full of awesome customers makes up for it.

Buy people drinks. Let your bartenders buy people drinks. Having awesome people frequent your bar attracts more awesome people. Having shitty people as regulars drives everyone else away.

Awesome begets awesome.

Shitty begets shitty.

Nobody wants to hang out with assholes.

## Internet Jukebox

A couple of places I worked had these. The music was unpredictable and often really shitty.

I had a decent crowd one afternoon, looking forward to a busy day, maybe $150 in tips and $700 in bar sales, if I got lucky. Two of the regulars decided to get into a contest to see who could play the worst song on the internet jukebox. Within the hour, they were the only two left in the room. The jukebox made more money than I did that afternoon, but the bar made almost none. (I made $10 in tips that day, and the bar made maybe $75.)

That was the day I learned that control of the jukebox selection is the key to setting the tone of the room. You really can't trust drunk people with unlimited music choices. It rarely goes well.

# Consistency

People always want me to have bands play. "We'll bring in 150 people that night! It'll be great! You'll make tons of money!"

Well, yeah. Maybe. I'll make a bundle that night, but what about every other night? I have a solid crew of regulars and repeat customers. They are there because they know what they can expect and they like it.

For example, a new person comes into the bar. The music is at a good level, and the crowd is lively but not obnoxious. The bartender is friendly, and the drinks are good but inexpensive. Perfect place.

That new person loves it.

The next time their friend comes into town to visit, they say, "Let's go to that place on the corner! It's perfect for hanging out and catching up."

They all walk into the bar that night, and some shitty punk band is playing in the corner, and the band's friends are wasted and obnoxious. Crap.

They go someplace else.

The next time that person wants to go out, they say, "Let's go to that place on the corner. Wait, do they have bands every Thursday? Or was that Friday? I don't know. Let's just go somewhere else."

So having a band play one night cost me a customer forever. And not just one. We are no longer on their mental list of places they like to go. The amount of revenue I've lost over the next year is at least ten times what I made by having that one band that one time.

Consistency is important. If you're going to be a venue, you need a band every night. Sports bars need to be sports bars all the time. If you're going to be a mellow neighborhood tavern, it needs to be a mellow tavern every night.

# 9

## Drink Basics

Here is a beginners' guide to the basics. I oversimplify because every region is different, every state is different, and every city and every bar is different. This guide is meant to be a starting point to your own self-education. You will eventually figure all this out on your own, but for now, knowing a little about this stuff can go a long way.

Beer, cocktails, or wine. That's pretty much it. Let me break it down for you.

## On Beer

Beer comes in two basic styles: lager and ale.

Lagers are the most popular mass-produced "macrobrew" beer in America (macrobrew = large scale; microbrew = small scale). Think Budweiser. Keystone Light. Miller High Life. Lagers are made with bottom-fermented yeast at a cooler temperature, giving them simpler, crisper flavors. They tend to have less ABV and lower IBU than ales.

ABV = alcohol by volume, measured as a percentage.

IBU = International Bitterness Units, measured on a scale of 1–100. Budweiser is around 10, Sierra Nevada Pale Ale is about 40, and IPAs can be anywhere from 50 to 130. IPAs sometimes go off the chart . . .

Ales are made with top-fermented yeast at room temperature, giving them more intense, complex flavors and higher ABV and IBU.

Macro ales include Sierra Nevada Pale Ale, Newcastle Brown Ale, and Killian's Irish Red.

Now, a word on macro lagers, also known as "cheap American swill." In Portland, we drink Pabst, Rainier, Olympia, and Hamm's. In Texas, it's Lone Star. In Pennsylvania, Yuengling. In Wisconsin, Leinenkugel's. Minnesota has Grain Belt, and upstate New York has Utica Club. Southern California drinks a lot of Tecate. America as a whole drinks Bud, Miller, and Coors.

When you hear the word *lager*, think "simple," or what most of America calls "beer."

With microbreweries popping up everywhere, the menu has become a bit more complicated.

Micro lagers are pretty much what you'd expect. Well-crafted, small-batch, bottom-fermented beer. Not hoppy or malty, they are a more delicious option than Budweiser, with usually higher ABV.

Micro ales, from low IBU to high, include session ales, golden ales, hefeweizens, amber ales, porters and stouts, pale ales, ESBs, and IPAs. (Note: This is an absolutely incomplete list but broken down for simplicity.)

## Smoother, Crisper

- **Session ale:** This means "you can have a long drinking session and still stand up." These are made for long days at the river or the BBQ. You can drink many of these and not lose your head.

- **Golden ale:** Perfect for lager lovers who want a little more crafted flavor than most macros will provide. Higher ABV than session.
- **Hefeweizen:** Unfiltered wheat beer. Delicious when served with an orange slice.

## Darker, Maltier, Sweeter

- **Amber ale and brown ale:** More flavorful than golden, with an amber or brown color and malty goodness. In my experience, brown ales tend to be sweeter than ambers.
- **Porter and stout:** While technically not ales, these delicious numbers needed a place on this list. Dark and creamy, they are often more available in winter than in summer. Porters and stouts tend to have less ABV than other micros. They can be delicious when layered with cider (snakebite) or a light pale ale like Bass (black and tan).

## Hoppier, More Bitter

- **Pale ale:** Some hops, a little bitterness, a touch of malt, but not too far in either direction. A good middle-of-the-road micro (and my favorite).
- **ESB:** Means "extra special bitter." More explanation necessary?
- **IPA:** When England colonized India, they would try to send beer there by ship. It took a lot longer than the beer would stay fresh, so they put hops in their pale ale barrels, as a preservative. This resulted in a complex, really hoppy brew. Turns out it was delicious. Hence, "India Pale Ale."

What you will find, through many enjoyable research sessions, is where your tastes lie in regard to lager versus ale, the IBU spectrum, the light-dark spectrum, the hoppy-malty spectrum, and your ABV limits.

Want to have one beer and head off to bed? Go for a higher ABV. Want to impress your date? Make the evening last forever and be able to maintain? Stick with session beers.

Sidenote on cider: The new gluten-free trend is all right. If everyone eats less bread and pasta, we will all be healthier. Just ask your naturopath.

But let's not confuse *gluten-free* with *low carb*.

A gluten-free diet tends to have fewer carbs, because there's a lot of carbs in wheat.

Cider doesn't have any gluten; it's not made with wheat like beer is. But it does have tons of sugar. Sugar = Carbs. Cider IS NOT BETTER FOR YOUR DIET THAN BEER.

If you want to get drunk and not get fat, vodka soda. No fruit. At my bar we call that a "skinny white bitch." Not everyone who drinks them is skinny, white, and bitchy, but every skinny white bitch drinks them.

## On Cocktails

There are a few basic ways to mix a drink. Most cocktails are derived from one of the following:

- **Shots:** *Straight*, *straight up*, *up*, *shot*, and *neat* all mean "without ice."
- **On the rocks:** This means served over ice.
- **Shot and a back:** This is a shot of liquor accompanied by a chaser served in separate glasses—basically, an unmixed highball. The chaser can be juice, soda, water, pickle juice, a small beer, whatever. For example, "Hornitos on the rocks with an orange juice back, please."
- **Highball:** One part liquor, one part mixer, served over

ice, sometimes garnished. Highballs are also known as "and" cocktails: gin and tonic, whiskey and Coke, vodka and cranberry juice. Feel free to specify your garnish. "Vodka soda with two lemons" is not being picky. "Vodka soda with two lemons and no seeds" is being picky. (Sidenote on vodka cran vs. Cape Cod: Please don't get in the habit of ordering a "Cape Cod." You sound like a jerk. Also, skip the "Cuba libre." Just say "rum and Coke with a lime" like a normal person. Nobody's impressed.)

I also consider the "breezes" to be highballs. Two-parters: liquor and juice.

- Sea breeze: Vodka, cran, and grapefruit
- Bay breeze: Vodka, cran, and pineapple
- Madras: Vodka, cran, and OJ

I have been bartending for twenty years, and just now I had to look these up to be sure which was which.

I don't actually recommend ordering them by their names, especially in dive bars. Almost every dive bar bartender will ask you to clarify anyway, because everyone mixes them up, including me. When someone orders a sea breeze, I say, "Vodka, cran, and . . . ?" Partly because I'm afraid you don't know, and partly because I'm afraid I don't know. I really just want you to receive the drink you think you are ordering.

"Vodka, cran, and grapefruit" is a perfectly acceptable order.

## Martinis

If you order a "martini," you will get a four-to-one ratio of gin to dry vermouth, garnished with an olive or a lemon twist, shaken or stirred. Since a martini is all liquor, it is totally worth the upcharge to order call instead of well. (See below, "Well vs. Call.")

You can modify this basic cocktail in the following ways:

- Vodka martini: Same as above but with vodka instead of gin

- Gibson: Same as a martini but with a cocktail onion garnish
- Wet: More vermouth
- Dry: Less vermouth
- Extra dry: No vermouth
- Dirty: Added olive juice or brine
- Stirred: Served mixed and cold, but with no ice and very little water (pretty much straight gin)
- Shaken: Chilled way cold and watered down a little (The ice breaks apart, leaving a layer of little magic frozen pieces floating on the top of the drink.)
- Up: Strained into a glass
- On the rocks: Strained into a glass of ice

There really is nothing quite like a well-made slightly dirty, dry, shaken Beefeater martini up. Tastes like heaven.

Sidenote: Don't know where to get the best martini in town? Look for the rainbow flag. In my experience, gay bars have that shit DOWN. So freaking delicious. (Shout-out to Madame DuMoore. Best martini I've ever had.)

Sidenote on dirty martinis: The olive "juice" that makes a martini dirty is actually (and I'm extrapolating here) bleachy hand sweat.

Yes. Yuck.

Olives are stored in brine, which is basically salt and vinegar. Maybe some spices, but not necessarily. The opening bartender takes some olives out of the jar, puts them into the storage tray for the day, and pours a little brine over them to keep them fresh.

Then, all day long, the bartender touches ashtrays, toilets, bleach buckets, limes, and cocaine-covered money that is moist with the butt sweat of the dirty hippie who gave it to him. And then grabs out an olive.

Don't get me wrong. The bartender washes his hands after everything. And I mean everything. After touching hippie money especially.

At the very least, he wipes his hands off on a towel that is soaked in bleach.

But he also puts his fingers into the brine to pull out the olive for your Bloody Mary. Or your martini.

The closing bartender takes the olives that are left and pours them, with the brine that has been used all day, back into the olive jar.

In some places, that jar will last a month or more.

That is a whole lot of hippie butt sweat. And bleach fingers. And probably some cherry juice from the next bin over in the condiment tray.

Vinegar and salt are used to brine the olives, to prevent anything nasty from growing in it. The olives are fine to eat, don't worry. But that doesn't mean that the brine makes a good addition to your gin.

So we're back to why you should order martinis at martini bars and highballs at dive bars.

Martini bars have brine specifically for dirty martinis. Some dive bars do too. My bar has a jar of "olive juice," which is a dirty martini mixer. Not brine, but actual juice of olive. It hasn't had any fingers in it. Ever. But still, our martinis are mediocre at best. It is a dive bar, after all.

Take care when ordering, my friend.

That shit's gross.

The term martini is also used to describe many other mostly liquor cocktails, much to the dismay of craft cocktail snobs. They hate it.

"Well, technically . . ."

Oh shut up and go wax your handlebar mustache, you douche.

## *Other Martini Variations*

- Manhattan: Rye whiskey and sweet vermouth, cherry garnish
- Gimlet: Gin and lime juice, lime garnish
- Kamikaze: Vodka, triple sec (and/or sugar), and lime juice, lime garnish
- Cosmopolitan: Vodka, triple sec (and/or sugar), lime juice and cranberry, lime garnish
- Lemon drop: Vodka, sugar (and/or triple sec) and lemon juice, lemon garnish, sugar rim

Kamikazes, cosmos, lemon drops, and the like should be ordered with the clarification of how you would like it served. "Kamikaze up" means in a martini glass (or a "bucket," where I work). "Kamikaze rocks" is over ice, and "kamikaze shot" is served, you guessed it, in a shot glass.

Sidenote: Triple sec is orange-flavored syrup. It tastes like artificial sweetener. I think it's gross. It should be used very sparingly, if at all. I don't think there is a drink in existence that requires more than a tiny splash of it, and whenever possible, I use actual sugar or simple syrup (sugar water) instead.

## Bloody Marys

The basic Bloody Mary ingredients are vodka, tomato juice, Worcestershire sauce, celery salt, pepper, and a lime garnish. Bloody Marys are best with a stalk of celery for stirring. Salted rim or no. Everybody has their own version, and in my opinion it has gotten a little out of control. I understand horseradish. I understand sesame seeds, pickled asparagus, and chili flakes.

But garnished with a slider on a stick? Bacon? Come on. Trying just a little bit too hard.

## *Other Bloody Mary Variations*

- Bloody Maria: Tequila instead of vodka
- Caesar: Clamato instead of tomato juice (Canadians are weird.)

## Margaritas

A basic margarita is tequila, lime juice, a splash of triple sec, and sour mix. As long as it has tequila, some citrus, some sweet, and some sour, it's a margarita.

I use tequila, muddled lemons and limes, sugar, and grapefruit juice. They're delicious, and there's no gross triple sec or sour mix.

## Well vs. Call

"Well" is in reference to the bottles kept near the ice well, which is the bartender's workstation. It is the cheapest liquor in the house and is used whenever the customer doesn't specify a brand of liquor.

"Call" is when you ask for a particular liquor by name.

Well = whiskey Coke, greyhound.

Call = Jack and Coke, Stoli Greyhound.

Sidenote: Any tequila that you can get for $7 a bottle (most wells) isn't actually tequila. It's cheap grain alcohol with artificial tequila flavor and caramel color. Same with cheap whiskey, vodka, gin, and rum. Pretty gross, and gives you one hell of a hangover.

## Long Island

Whenever anyone orders a Long Island from me, my first reaction is to reinspect their ID.

"What? You just looked at it twenty seconds ago!"

Yeah, but anyone who's actually over twenty-one should know better.

A Long Island is a mix of the worst kind. Four different well liquors blended together—that's about a shot and a half of cheap grain alcohol and four different artificial flavors and colors. Yuck. They are so gross you have to put a shot of triple sec in there too to hide the flavor. Then add more sugar water (or sour mix, which is fake citrus flavor mixed with sugar) and a splash of Coke so it looks brown. To order a Long Island is to tell the bartender that you (a) heard once that they get you drunk and that you think it's "cool" to be the guy who gets wasted and therefore (b) are going to be a problem within the hour.

## Drop Shots

A drop shot is a shot glass of liquor dropped into a half-full pint glass of mixer. Intended for chugging.

- Boilermaker: Whiskey shot in lager
- Irish car bomb: Jameson and Baileys dropped in Guinness
- Jäger bomb: Jägermeister dropped in Red Bull
- Flaming Dr Pepper: Amaretto with a float of 151, lit on fire and dropped into lager

I'd leave the drop shots to the club. No dive bar bartender wants to clean up your puke. Also, I recard when people order these. Nobody ever does these unless they have a fake ID or just turned twenty-one yesterday. Drink these where there's a janitor on duty. Please.

## Flavored vs. Infused

*Flavored* liquor is liquor that has artificial flavoring added to it by the distillery. Like Absolut Mandarin or Stoli Blueberi.

*Infused* means someone took a bottle of vodka (or whatever) and let it sit for a month with something in it to add to the flavor.

This process is done by the bar itself, to add something to a specialty drink, as opposed to flavored liquor, which is bought that way.

## On Wine

Okay, so, I don't know anything about wine. And even if I did, there is no real way to simplify it. There are books, classes, even master's degrees on the subject. Anyway, most dive bars have a choice of red or white. One of each. Pretty straightforward.

## Spritzers

Spritzers are wine mixed with soda, 7Up, juice, or any combination of the three. These can be delicious and a good way to choke down cheap bar wine.

## Champagne Cocktails

Pretty obviously, these are cocktails made with champagne as a mixer. A mimosa, for example. My favorite is champagne, lemonade, and a tiny splash of St-Germain Elderflower Liqueur. So good. And not just for breakfast.

# Notes

# 10

## On Ordering

**Q:** What's the cheapest thing in here?
**A:** Right now? You are.

**Q:** What's good here?
**A:** The service, if I am allowed to provide it instead of standing here answering stupid questions.

**Q:** Make it a good one.
**A:** Sure. I always go out of my way to give free shit to people who insult me to my face.

This last one has to be the absolute worst thing I hear as a bartender. And it happens. A lot.

When someone says that to me, this is what I hear: "Hi. You don't know me, and I don't know you. Despite this fact, I assume you make terrible drinks and are really bad at your job. You suck. I'm sure that if I hadn't said anything, you would, of course, make a weak drink. Having made my opinion of you very clear, I would really like you to put your livelihood in jeopardy by stealing from the company that employs you. Obviously, even though I am a total asshole, I'm sure that I deserve more booze than everyone else. How else am I supposed to become a problem for you later? I want you to do this for me, because you are just a lowly servant, and your job is to kiss my ass. Also, I'm very likely not going to tip you."

This "make it a good one" statement usually comes with a finger gun and a *chk-chk* cheek clicking sound. The douchey-est.

So . . .

This is how I "make it a good one" for you.

I pour my regular shot. They're pretty hefty to begin with, but for effect, I go a little overboard. And then I grab the jigger. The jigger is the silver hourglass thing that craft cocktail makers use to get proportions right. It's a liquor measuring cup.

I take the huge shot I just poured for you and measure it into the one-ounce side of the jigger, filling it exactly. I then, in front of you and whatever friend you were trying to impress by asking for a good one in the first place, pour the rest into the bar mat and return the one-ounce shot to your glass.

You want a good shot?

Here. This one's so good IT'S PERFECT.

That'll be $5, please.

Let me clarify a little. There's nothing wrong with wanting a strong drink. There is, however, something wrong with assuming my drinks are weak when you've never had one. There is also something wrong with asking me to do you a favor that constitutes stealing from my boss, especially after insulting me to my face, in front of all my other customers. You think you are being smooth. But you really are being an asshole.

The other thing that bothers me about that scenario is that you're implying that you will refuse to pay me for my service unless I give you free stuff. And if I don't, you'll most likely complain about me behind my back. It's just shitty. "This drink is so weak! Can you imagine how weak it would have been if I hadn't asked for a strong one? This bartender sucks!"

Actually, jerkface, it would have been an excellent drink if you had just trusted me to know my job and do it well.

Imagine if I were a bank teller and someone pointed a finger gun at me and told me to give him extra money in his withdrawal. He would likely get arrested. And I would be right to sound the alarm, if only to make a point. That point is, YOU ARE NOT AS FUNNY AS YOU THINK YOU ARE.

Please, please, please just try your drink before complaining about its strength. If your whiskey Coke doesn't taste strong enough for you, order it "with just a splash" next time. ("Whiskey on the rocks with a splash of Coke.")

"Jameson and ginger, and heh-heh, light on the ice, if you know what I mean, heh-heh." (Don't forget the finger gun, *chk-chk*.)

Shots of liquor are measured out. Sometimes with a jigger, but usually by the skill and professionalism of the bartender. The rest of the drink is variable, but a shot is a shot is a shot. Every drink has the same amount of liquor in it. Less ice in your drink just means more room for the mixer. You think you are asking for a stronger drink, but what you really are ordering is a weaker-tasting one. Same amount of Jameson, more ginger ale. Here's a quick guide:

- Tall glass = More mixer (tastes weaker)
- Less ice = More mixer
- A splash = Less mixer (tastes stronger)
- Lots of ice = Less mixer

No variation on the amount of anything else that goes into the drink means "more liquor," except "double," and it is double the price. That's just the way it is.

Please have your money ready. The amount of time it takes for me to make your round should suffice for you to pull out your wallet. The line is growing behind you.

My pet peeve, and least-favorite time waster, is when I pour someone a cheap pint of beer and they have a $20 in their hand, all nice and ready. I reach for it, thankful that I don't have to wait for the wallet to be found in the purse before I can complete the transaction and move on. But then the customer pulls it back, out of reach, and says, "How much is it?"

Well, I promise you one thing. It's less than $20. Just hand that shit over and let's move on.

I can only figure the reason for this baffling behavior is people think if they know beforehand how much the beer is, it will somehow prevent me from giving wrong change or stealing from or overcharging them.

If I wanted to overcharge you, making me say the price I'm charging out loud would not prevent me from doing so.

I get it. If you have ordered a full round of drinks, $20 may not be enough. But I'll tell you what. Pulling that $20 out of the reach of the bartender isn't going to help at all. Just hand it over. If I need more than you've given me, I promise I will let you know.

**Q:** What do you like to make?
**A:** A drink for the guy patiently waiting behind you in line.

Eye contact should equal an order. Once you have the attention of the bartender, you have about five seconds. If you have not decided yet, you will lose your turn. (This doesn't mean you are now at the end of the line. This means the bartender will do something else while you decide. Maybe serve someone else. Maybe stock the cooler. Whatever she needs done. She will come back to you, I promise.)

**Q:** Just a second, I'm on the phone.
**A:** Yeah. I see. Hang up or get the fuck out of the way.

I can't believe people still do this. But they do. They are talking on the phone while in line, and when they get to the front, they decide to stand there and finish their conversation.

Sometimes they will turn sideways to signal that they aren't talking to me but will continue to stand in the order well to keep their place in line.

THE NERVE OF THOSE PEOPLE. Really. Who raised you???

I have no qualms about politely pushing them to the side and serving the person behind them. Sometimes they get pissed and confused, but I decided long ago that if someone can't recognize that in dealing with bartenders, basic rules of tact apply, then I don't really want them in my bar anyway. Let them get pissed. Maybe I will be spared their repeat business.

I recommend having a backup drink. A simple highball that you know you like, and you know every liquor bar can make. Many bars don't serve certain types of drinks; for example, at my bar we don't do drop shots or have energy drinks. (We don't have a bouncer. It really doesn't work for us to have a bunch of people in the bar hopped up AND wasted.) So if Jäger bombs are your thing and when you order one the bartender says, "Sorry, we don't do those here," you have something else that just rolls off your tongue. "Oh? Okay. How about just a Jack and Coke, then." Getting into a philosophical discussion with the bartender about why they don't have Red Bull is not going to change the fact that they don't have Red Bull. Please order something else.

**Q:** Can I get a cranberry vodka?

**A:** Sorry. We don't have cranberry. We have blueberry, vanilla, and mandarin.

When this happens, they look at me like I'm stupid.

I'm not.

"You don't have cranberry juice? What kind of bar doesn't have cranberry juice?"

Of course we have cranberry juice. We do not, however, have cranberry vodka.

A song came out a couple of years ago called "Cranberry Vodka" by iLLA. The "cranberry vodka" part is repeated over and over and over. Now almost everyone who wants a vodka and cranberry orders a cranberry vodka.

This is the truth of the matter: To order a "cranberry vodka" is to ask for a warm well shot of cranberry-flavored vodka, or infused, if it's that kind of place. A "vodka cranberry" is a highball. Ice, vodka, and cranberry juice, often garnished with lime.

Now, I'm not saying this is iLLA's fault. I actually watched the music video, and a bottle of Absolut flavored vodka makes an appearance. He's talking about a champagne cocktail. Champagne mixed with flavored vodka. Yum.

He has it right. It's everyone else who's screwing it up.

When ordering a highball, the liquor comes first. Whiskey Coke, gin and tonic, vodka cranberry. The bartender almost always pours the liquor first, so if he's barely started making it and you decide you want orange juice instead of cranberry, it's okay to change your mind. But if you decide you want Grey Goose instead of well, sorry. It's too late.

**Q:** What do you have on tap?

**A:** (with a Vanna White wave across the tap handles that are right in front of you) Other than these?

Nothing.

Then, to avoid seeming (or being) too bitchy, I will ask, "Can you see them?" Because, you know, sometimes people don't wear their glasses.

I also offer to describe some of them, but only after I've asked you what kind of beer you like. If I take the time to go down the entire row of twelve tap handles and describe the nuances of flavor inherent in each one while the line backs up behind you, you will ALWAYS order a Budweiser. ALWAYS.

There is a really easy way to get a beer you will like.

Ask.

This doesn't mean ask, "What's good?" or "What do you like?" or, the worst, "What will I like?" I really hate that one.

"I tend to like ambers or browns, malty beers. Got anything like that?"

You will get an amber or a brown, or the bartender will say, "We have a local seasonal that's a little malty and pretty tasty. How about one of those?"

My beer order in a new place where I don't see anything I know I like on tap goes like this: "I like pale ales, something a little hoppy and not malty." Or, "Got anything that's hoppy but not obnoxiously so?" I usually get something I can enjoy.

Go ahead and ask for a little taste. If it's busy, I will pour a little sample or two and go serve someone else while you decide, or catch up on some dishes or whatever. When I come back, you'll have tasted them and made up your mind. It may be a minute or two from when you stepped up to the bar until you have a drink in your hand. This is totally fine. I've got plenty to do, and I haven't forgotten your place at the front of the line. It's sixteen ounces of commitment, after all, and I really just want you to enjoy your beer.

But . . . if you plan on taking my attention the whole time while deciding, that's not okay. Also, if I walk away while you taste, that doesn't mean I am ignoring you. It just means that there are seventy-five customers in the room and only one bartender. I got shit to do!

**Q:** Can I have a Kentucky Mind Fuck?
**A:** No. Weirdly, I don't actually know what's in the drink you and your friends made up last night at your house.

This happens more often than my faith in humanity is happy with.

People actually, seriously, expect me to know how to make a drink that some bartender friend of theirs in Texas made up and put on the drink menu at their local tavern. Or the one they made up at their party last week. Or one that they dreamed about once last summer.

It's baffling. The worst part is how they look at me, surprised that I am still employed as a bartender, given my obvious lack of knowledge on the subject. What kind of bartender are you, anyway? I thought you were supposed to know drinks. You have ONE JOB . . .

Remember this: Every bartender ever has made up and named at least one drink. That's a whole lot of unheard-of cocktails. Some catch on, like Colorado Bulldog, for example, and most bartenders know what it is. But with nonstandards, if you want a particular cocktail, it really is your responsibility to know how to make it. (Colorado Bulldog = White Russian with a splash of Coke.) But very few "made up on a boring Monday night" cocktails make it past Tuesday.

We don't share a hive mind or go to conventions. There's no way I can know what the hell you're talking about.

Also, if you're so proud of this drink you invented, shouldn't you know how to make it? Just tell me.

I'll do my very best to reproduce it for you, and if it's good, it may even end up on the drink menu.

# 11

## On Tipping

"Why do I have to give you a dollar every time you open a can of beer? I don't make a dollar every time I do twenty seconds of work!"

Here's a story. And every word is true.

Once upon a time, there was a regular at a tavern I worked at in my twenties named Ganda. (Her parents were Tolkien fans. Ganda was short for Gandalf. Interesting and sort of tragic, but totally irrelevant to this story.)

Tequila and OJ, usually five to six in a sitting, three to four times a week.

One particularly memorable evening she waved me aside to share a revelation with me. She seemed pretty proud of it.

"I sat here last night and watched you constantly stuff dollar bills into your tip pitcher. You guys make a lot of money, more than me, so I have decided I am no longer going to tip a dollar a drink. I'm going to tip a dollar every two or three drinks. Just a heads-up. If you don't get a tip from me, it doesn't mean you're doing a bad job. I work hard for my money, and I don't see how putting ice, tequila, and some juice in a glass merits a whole dollar every time."

This is the story I told her. And now I'm gonna tell you.

Here's my day at work so far.

Last night, after you left, Maury was at the bar, having an especially incoherent evening, and shat himself in the very chair you chose to occupy today. I mean, it was epic. He released a lifelong-alcoholic-failing-liver-liquid-diet-spray, all leaking out his khaki pants. Greenish, dripping, and putrid. As soon as I got his foul ass out the door and sent him home to his crappy apartment across the street, I took the chair out to the alley, hosed it off, and left it to air. It was sorta busy (albeit less busy after the smell made itself known), so I left it there until morning.

Sidenote: My boss at the time would not allow me to cut off the "old regulars." Left to my own devices, and empowered to make those decisions myself, Maury would have been sent home hours earlier.

Good morning! Today my first job upon arriving was to pull out the rubber gloves, the bleach, and the hose.

I bleached the chair, rinsed it down, and bleached it again. I dried it off, smelled it (eeeeeeewwwwww) to make sure there was no more feces left in any of the crevices, and decided, just to be safe, to bleach and rinse it again.

Man, was I glad when that was over.

I put it back at the bar and began prepping for a busy afternoon.

While cutting the limes, I heard some noise coming from the bathroom hallway. I looked up and saw a junkie, looking freshly fixed up, stumbling his way out the door and shrugging half-apologetically at me. Damn.

How the hell did he get past me? Oh yeah. I was busy hosing human waste off the furniture.

Now, a little known fact (little known to everybody but dive bar bartenders) is that a sneaky junkie never, ever, EVER leaves a bar bathroom nicer than he found it. Law of nature.

So.

I took a deep breath and went into the men's room.

SURPRISE!

Nothing out of place!

That was close. I didn't think after my episode with the chair I could handle whatever surprise he might have left for me. Whew. While there, I figured I might as well get it ready for the day. Stock toilet paper, soap, and hand towels. Scrub the toilet and sink. You get the picture.

*Whistle while you work! Try to erase the "Maury shit chair" experience from your memory, Tanya! This gag reflex has to relax some if I'm gonna make it through this shift. It's gonna be a good afternoon—I can convince myself of that, right? Mind over matter. Power of positive thinking! Can't let a little poop ruin a whole day!*

I figured I had better attend to the women's room. It's usually not as gross as the men's. Messier, sure. But not as gross. Really, the worst part's over! All uphill from here!

NOOOOOOOOOOOOOOO!!!!!!!!

(Something else I should mention is that sneaky junkies don't usually follow the gender signs on bathroom doors either. Double damn.)

JUNKIE BLOOD SPRAY!!!!!

ALL. OVER.

Walls, ceiling, toilet paper dispenser, sink, floor.

Wow. So much for the power of positive thinking.

Hello, rubber gloves and bleach! My old comrades in battle.

Throw out the TP, take the dispenser off the wall. Throw out all the paper towels, take that dispenser off the wall too. Trash cans, toilet seat, floor, ceiling. Soak in bleach. Scrub, bleach, scrub. Rinse. Repeat.

Awesome.

This day so far rules. (Can you smell that sarcasm?)

I can't believe I get paid a whole $2.19 an hour for doing this awesome, satisfying work.

Fast-forward a couple of hours. You, Ganda, have a spot at the bar. You go to the bathroom and leave your purse, open, with cash showing, sitting right there on the bar.

Enter sketchy dude, who had been on my radar in the neighborhood as someone to keep an eye on. I saw him notice the cash and oh-so-sneakily look around for its owner. (Okay, not so sneakily, but at least he tried.)

I moved around the bar to have a chat with him, but before I could say, "Please, sir, find somewhere else to be," he started reaching for the cash and preparing to bolt. I grabbed him by his wrist before he reached it.

Words, insults . . . things that would get edited out anyway. I've been called a lot of things in my lifetime, and usually by jerks like this one. But I remember this tirade especially. Pretty nasty.

I managed to get him out the door without getting punched. That in itself was a miracle.

At this point, you returned from the bathroom and promptly took the opportunity to reveal to me your grand, new tipping plan, complete with how I don't do enough for you to earn your precious dollar.

I JUST DON'T DO ENOUGH FOR YOU TO EARN ONE DOLLAR.

So, Ganda. I want you, when you come back from the no-junkie-blood bathroom, to sit on your no-Maury-shit chair, to reach into that purse, which is exactly where you left it, and which miraculously still has a pile of cash in it . . .

and GIVE ME A DAMN DOLLAR!

The moral of this story, in case you missed it: When tipping a bartender, especially in a dive bar, you are not giving her a dollar to throw some booze and mixer in a glass. Or open a can of beer or whatever. That's what we get paid $2.19 an hour for. (WHEE!)

What the dollar a drink is for is this: You go to a bar to be social. Drink, listen to the jukebox. Play pool. Pinball. What have you. But mostly to be social in a safe environment. One that you don't have to clean up yourself. Or monitor. Or prep.

If you're only there for the beer, go to 7-Eleven, pick up a six-pack, and go home. Your cat can keep you company.

The dollar is for everything that comes with that drink, and everything that happens for you in the hour or so that you're drinking it. Let's run through these, in no particular order.

## Ambience

The mood of the room is tightly controlled by the bartender. Music loud enough that you can hear, but not so loud that you can't have a conversation. The bartender is constantly adjusting volume. More people = more voices = volume needs to go up to hear the music over the conversation. But not too much, because louder music = louder voices = too loud to hear what your friend is saying to you. It's a delicate balance, and one that takes attention and experience to reach.

Someone plays a song on the jukebox that was recorded at a different level than the rest? Bartender notices and adjusts accordingly. Someone unknowingly (or really more likely on purpose, because people are kinda jerks when they think they're being funny) plays the hidden track with a half hour of silence followed by a screechy, deafening baby crying? Did you notice that? No?

That's because I skipped that song before it happened.

# General Maintenance and Service

Here to play pinball? Yep. They ALL broke yesterday, but don't worry. I fixed it. Or called the guy to fix it for me.

Need money at the ATM? It actually did run out this morning. But there's money in it now!

Need matches? A couple of Advil? A charger for your phone? Some orange juice for your low blood sugar? A pen and some paper? A roll of quarters so you can do your laundry?

No problem.

# Bathrooms

Bar bathrooms are disgusting by nature. The bartender attends to all manner of nasties. Constantly.

Mopping urine off the floor.

Pulling puke chunks out of the sink. Bleaching the toilet, then making sure the bleach is rinsed off so you don't ruin your clothes.

Throughout any shift, the bartender cleans, stocks, fixes, and monitors the bathrooms. So you can piss in peace and don't have to wait too long, because the bartender also notices someone monopolizing the room, doing drugs, or having sex. Or passed out. Or looking for privacy for a phone call. (Really, dude? There are 150 people in here and one bathroom. Get the hell outta there and go sit in a corner to finish your conversation. Jeez.)

Or drawing graffiti. Or fighting with their friend. Whatever the deal, the bartender keeps the line moving.

# Crowd Monitoring

While serving drinks, keeping track of tabs, and monitoring the music and the bathrooms and everything else, one of the more important functions of the bartender is crowd control.

Douchebag relentlessly hitting on girls who'd rather be left alone? Bartender either distracts him (throwing herself on the douche grenade, as it were) or just plain kicks him out.

Wasted girl who needs more attention than she's getting? Trying to sit on everybody's lap? Being an annoying nuisance? Bartender sends her home with her friends.

"Can I bum a cigarette? Spare change?" Doesn't happen. Bartender has already shuffled them out the door with a smile.

Got a glass with lipstick residue on it? Sorry. I guess I missed that one. But the other four glasses you used tonight at one point had lipstick on them too. I got those ones. Nobody's perfect. I didn't see that particular one because while I was washing that load of dishes, a wasted, bummy-type guy was outside, contemplating coming in to sit at your table until you gave him a dollar to go away. I stopped washing the dishes to go to the door to convince him to go someplace else. It worked.

Feel free to give me that dollar I just saved you instead. (P.S. If the lipstick smear didn't come off in the 250-degree high-pressure dishwasher, it's not going to come off in your whiskey.)

Dude orders four shots and drinks them all in twenty minutes? Did you get puked on? Did he fall onto your table, knocking your date's drink in her lap? Did he get in a fight with your friend so now you have to get involved—you know, bro code or whatever?

No?

Wanna know why?

Bartender handled it. When she realized he intended to drink all four shots himself, she stopped him after the second one. Took the third and fourth away from him. She got called names. Thief, cunt, whatever. "I'm telling your boss!" "I'm gonna get you fired!" "I know my rights!" "You gonna make me?" And my personal favorite, "IT'S A FREE COUNTRY!" (Actually, no, it's not, buddy. It's a democracy. And the rest of us have a problem with what you're doing.)

Somehow she got him out the door without making a scene and into a cab. With a smile and a helping hand. Maybe even cab fare. (Did you know we do that? Sometimes we pay for cabs for people who are being jerks to us. Name one other profession where workers pay out of their own pocket to help someone who is trying to punch them. Bet you can't. Okay, maybe cops or teachers. Sometimes. But only the ones who are angels.)

If she's good at her job, then nobody saw it happen.

# Information

Your bartender knows so very much about you, most of which is unknown to the general public. Although, technically, there isn't "client privilege," the bartender-customer relationship is almost shrink-like and is based on mutual trust.

We could totally use it for evil, but we consider it our sacred professional responsibility to keep our sober, watchful eyewitness accounts of all the dumb shit people do to ourselves. Unless, of course, harm would come from silence.

Meeting a potential client for a drink? How about I don't say, "Welcome back! That's the third time today you've walked through my door. To what do I owe the pleasure?"

Mom in town? How about I don't bring up your delinquent bar tab in front of her?

On a date with a classy-looking lady? How about I don't ask you how it went that one time you asked that girl to give you a BJ in the alley?

Got a girlfriend? How about I don't tell her how I saw you hitting on someone else yesterday?

Got three different guys you went home with at one time or another all sitting at the bar? How about I don't say, "Ya know what? You guys have more in common than you think!"

We don't ever look down on you, shame you, lecture you, or treat you differently. It's a matter of pride for us. And a measure of our professionalism.

You're welcome.

We hope you had a good time at our bar today, and we look forward to seeing you soon.

That is what the dollar a drink is for. I usually tip $2.

# 12

## Misconceptions

There are a few things that people feel bad about that they really shouldn't.

### Tipping in Change

I hear this a lot. "I'm sorry there's change in my tip. I know I shouldn't do that. Bartenders hate it."

No. No, we don't.

We hate it when your change is $1.50, and you take the dollar and leave us the $0.50.

We hate it when you take your paper dollar change from your order, put it away, and then dig for three quarters to throw on the bar.

But if your change is $1.50 and you leave us the whole $1.50, we think it's AWESOME. Especially when we know that the alternative is for you to take the $0.50 and just leave us the dollar. At the end of the night all those extra quarters add up to real money.

Two dollars in quarters is a way better tip than a one-dollar bill.

There was a club in Portland where the bartenders were required by management to throw any change they received at the customer who left it for them.

I probably don't need to add that this particular club is now out of business. That's just plain stupid, not to mention really rude.

A dollar a drink is standard. Anything above that is awesome, no matter what form it takes.

## Playing the Jukebox When the Bartender Is Playing Their Own Music or the Television

We play our music for background because we know that silence kinda sucks when you're in a bar.

We do get sick of our own choices and are grateful to you for switching it up a little. Also, the bar makes money on the jukebox. Encouraging people to use it is part of our job.

WE LOVE IT.

The television is a little trickier. If *Law & Order* is playing with the sound on, you can be pretty sure it's okay to play the juke, as long as you let the bartender know your intention so they can mute the TV. If it's "THE GAME" or something that the whole bar is into, it's probably not okay to take over the room with your choice of music.

Feel free to ask. Usually we are stoked. "YES! Please play some music! I'm sick of the television being on. THANK YOU and here's an extra dollar jukebox subsidy."

# After Hours

Sometimes the bartender wants to have a drink after work, if they are allowed by management to do so. Usually we want to have a buddy to sit and chat with after a long shift.

The misconception is that there's a party every night. I'm sure this is true in some places and for some bartenders. But a lot of the time, silence and solitude are what we really want more than anything.

If you have been invited to stay, you may be expected to work a little. Put up the chairs, wipe tables, wash ashtrays.

Remember, this is the chance for the bartender to unwind after work. Please don't ask her to make you a martini. Or anything, really. You should be serving her.

The negative side of this, for the bartender, is that now your buddy will try to stay every single time. Just because you stayed once, or even a hundred times, PLEASE don't assume you are automatically welcome. If I am asking everybody to go, that means you too. Don't linger. Don't start putting chairs up.

Unless I ask if you want to have a drink with me after work, I don't want any company. I shouldn't have to say, "Not tonight. You actually do have to leave." If you make me say that to you, I will probably not invite you again.

# 13
## Douche Moves

## Douche Move 1: Bringing your own alcohol into a bar.

"I bought this!"

Not from me, asshole.

What do you think we do here? Provide a service where someone cleans up after you for free? They have those—they're called "Mom."

"What's the big deal? It doesn't cost you anything to have me here. Why you gotta be such a bitch?"

Okay, people. Here's what the big deal is.

If you serve yourself (this is also why we have to open the can we serve you; if YOU open it, you technically are serving yourself), the bartender gets fired, and (in Oregon, at least) the fine they have to pay can be up to $4,000. The bar owner has to pay twice that much.

The bartender, and the bar itself, is liable for everything you do. If you drink at the bar and then go out and kill someone with your car, the bar can be held liable whether we served you or not. Accessory to murder. Vehicular homicide. JAIL.

You hear me?

I GO TO JAIL.

Or at the very least have to pay a steep fine and lose my license to serve alcohol. I lose my job and can never work as a bartender again unless I move to another state.

For some shit YOU did. For you feeling sneaky and saving yourself two dollars. For something I have no control over. For you getting drunk on booze that I didn't serve you and had to clean up after you and didn't get paid for.

"I bought this beer, so even though I've been sipping out of my flask, you can't kick me out until I've finished the drink I paid for."

WRONG AGAIN.

If you are breaking the law, for which I am liable, putting me, my boss, and my coworkers at risk for fines or worse, then I can take your beer and all your friends' beer and ask you to leave. In fact, what I'm supposed to do is call the police. It's the only thing that can really protect me from being screwed by your actions. You should be kissing my ass that I don't have you arrested for trespassing and theft.

(The second I ask you to leave and you don't, you are trespassing. If you are receiving a service that we charge for and you didn't pay for it, you are stealing.)

"Fuck you, cunt! I'll get you fired!"

That's right. Fuck me, cunt.

Go ahead and call my boss, your lawyer, the cops, WHATEVER.

I'm right and you're wrong. If you want to battle about it, you will lose.

Go away and never come back.

# Douche Move 2: Drawing graffiti.

There's graffiti in bar bathrooms. That's great. We all love to read it.

"So-and-so loves so-and-so forever."

Cute. Slightly annoying. But fine. As long as there's other graffiti there, go ahead and write your piece.

However, if there is no graffiti, don't feel like the world needs to hear your most genius thought.

"I'm sick and tired of taking a shit. Next time I think I'll leave one."

The poor bartender, janitor, maintenance person, or bar owner who has to come in to work on their day off to paint over that idiotic statement really hates you.

We all need to understand the difference between writing on a $25 table that is already covered in graffiti or in a bathroom that encourages expression and writing on a mural that the bar paid an artist $2,000 to paint. Not to mention how rude it is to tag someone's art.

Or the wooden patio wall that is thus far graffiti-free. That Sharpie doesn't come out of the wood. I can't paint over it. I have to replace it at $75 an hour for carpenter labor plus the price of the materials. Your shitty drawing cost me a lot of money.

I HAVE to fix it. I can't just leave it. If there's ONE piece of graffiti, everyone thinks it's fine to tag. My awesome bar would become a shitty, uncomfortable place to hang out in a matter of weeks.

When people are in a place that obviously isn't respected by the clientele, they will also disrespect it. It all goes to shit.

A little bit of common sense and respect goes a really long way.

# Douche Move 3: Aw guuurrl, those tits are NICE!

Never in a million years would a dude say that to me and expect not to get kicked out immediately.

But you're not a dude, so it's okay, right? We're all girls here!

I get it. We're all empowered women. You're a modern girl. Good for you. So am I. We are both comfortable with our bodies, proud of our awesome breasts. We wear clothes that accent our best features. We buck against the societal pressure to be ashamed of our sexuality by highlighting the very things that make us sexually desirable.

I took that class in college too.

But look here, little girl.

I am at work. The bar is lined with men who are trying so very hard not to stare at my rack. For the most part, they succeed, but when they fail, I don't mind so terribly much, as long as they respect me. I am in a position of authority, and in their minds, I am off-limits.

The second you say, "Look at her tits!" I am transformed from "professional, efficient, funny, hardworking lady who serves me great drinks" to "Man, I hope she bends over! What a view!"

Thanks a lot.

P.S. Yes, I have tattoos where you can't see them. And no, you can't see them.

P.S.S. No, I don't want a hug.

# Douche Move 4: Playing videos on your laptop or phone with the sound on.

I get it. You're here to have a good time and hang out with your friends. But you need to remember that so is everybody else.

If having a good time means doing shit that annoys everybody around, you should have had a party at your house instead.

One obnoxious group having a great time together can easily empty out a full bar. The bartender should have no hesitation about shaming that group into silence or sending them on their way.

When I have to raise my voice so my friend can hear what I'm saying over the video you're playing on your laptop, or am simply distracted, I have stopped having a good time. It's like when someone has a conversation on their cell phone while standing in line at the bank. IT'S ANNOYING. Bring your headphones if you want to hear it. That shit's obnoxious.

P.S. If you and all your friends want to have a romping good time singing "Livin' on a Prayer" at the top of your lungs, the karaoke bar is right around the corner. If we wanted to hear you sing, we would have gone there. If you wanted to sing, you should've gone there too.

## Douche Move 5: It's my birthday! I get a free shot!

No. No, you don't.

How many times have you asked a total stranger to buy you something? Why do you think it's okay if that total stranger happens to be a bartender?

If I've never seen you before and you walk up to me and say, "Gimme free shit. It's my birthday," I will decide that you are a little entitled snot and I don't really want you in the bar. Why would I give you free drinks? Why would I do anything to encourage you and your obviously cheap friends to hang out? If they're not willing to buy you a drink, why should I?

If you are in the bar district of your town and decide to go from bar to bar to bar demanding free drinks, you will fail.

Your birthday will suck, because every place you go will think you are an asshole.

We do have some leeway to buy drinks on the house for people. We save those for people we like, appreciate, and want to come back again.

I will give drinks on the house to strangers if they (a) don't demand that I do, (b) are well behaved, (c) tip well, and (d) are the kind of person whom I want to have as a repeat customer.

Pretty much takes points *a*, *b*, and *c* to make a *d*.

Get over yourself. I don't give one sparkly flying fuck about your birthday.

I, however, am a professional.

If you behave like the type of person I want to frequent my establishment, I will do whatever is in my power to convince you that you've found your new favorite bar.

That includes buying you drinks for your birthday.

Douche Move 6: Having a bachelorette party at a gay club.

"HEY, EVERYBODY! I'm getting married! America voted last week to deny you that right, but I'm straight, so I get to. YAY!"

"Buy me a shot??? How about a lap dance???"

Gay bars are fun. No doubt.

Adversity breeds character, and being gay in America puts plenty of adversity in your path. Nobody knows how to have a great time like gay people do. And there are hot dude strippers!

But whatever you do, straights, remember you are part of the oppressor class. And on the turf of the oppressed.

If you want to have a wedding party at a gay club, go out and make it legal for gays to marry. Vote. Get active.

Then, after all of your hard work for equality has paid off and gay marriage is legal, and only then, can you celebrate your straight wedding on gay turf.

Until that happens, you're just being a self-absorbed, entitled asshole.

Vote, please. And don't rub your right to marry in the faces of those to whom you deny that very right.

P.S. To all the girls who go to gay clubs to avoid getting hit on . . .

It's cool. Gay clubs are fun and generally full of nice people. It's true they won't hit on you. Have fun, dance, maybe make a new friend.

But going up to a stranger and saying, "Will you be my gay boyfriend?" is just plain rude. These guys go to gay clubs, in part, to avoid being hit on by women. Claiming a stranger as your new pet is just shitty. He's not there to get a new fag hag. He's there to meet other gay men.

Just leave him to it. Better yet, if you don't want to get hit on by dudes, go out to the straight club in your Hello Kitty sweatpants. I promise the guys will leave you alone to get your dance on in peace.

Douche Move 7: "It's a service dog. You have to let it in!"

You are right. I do have to let service dogs in. But I can refuse service to any person for any reason.

Bringing in your poorly behaved pet and claiming it's a service animal is reason enough for me to ask you to leave.

You can leave the dog here, though. We will find it a good home.

The Americans with Disabilities Act (ADA) defines a service animal as "a dog that has been individually trained to do work or perform tasks for an individual with a disability. The task(s) performed by the dog must be directly related to the person's disability." The ADA also states, "The dog must be trained to take a specific action when needed to assist the person with a disability." If they meet this definition, animals are considered service animals under the ADA regardless of whether they have been licensed or certified by a state or local government.

A service animal is not a pet.

A companion animal is not a service animal.

Yes, I have to allow service dogs in the bar. I don't mind this at all. Service dogs are totally awesome, well behaved, and helpful to their owners. I LOVE THEM.

On the other hand, the health department gives me a pretty steep fine if they find a pet dog in the bar. I also don't mind this law at all. Most dogs that people try to bring into the bar are annoying, smelly, and poorly behaved. They need constant monitoring, and their owners are usually oblivious to how their dog is bothering everybody else. I DON'T LOVE THEM.

The problem comes when people bring their mutt into the bar and try to sell me on the *idea* that it's a "service dog."

Yeah, right. You mean that dog that just took a shit on the floor?

REALLY. A service dog.

Every single one of them pulls out a piece of paper, printed off the internet. "Look! I've got papers!"

Here's a news flash: Real service dogs don't have paperwork. In fact, it's illegal for me to ask you for proof. Whatever asshole sold you that piece of paper is a scam artist and you fell for it.

But it is legal for me to kick your ass out, and your dog too, if I don't believe it's a service dog.

(Which I figured out the second you walked in with your dog's hemp-rope leash dragging behind him.)

Or if I just plain don't like you.

(Which I figured out the second you tried to play yourself off as "disabled" so you could get special treatment.)

You now fall into the same category as able-bodied people who somehow got a handicapped parking permit so they can park closer at Olive Garden.

"It's the law!! I'll sue!"

Go ahead, scummy hippie. If you can't afford shoes, you can't afford a $25,000 service animal. Or a lawyer, for that matter.

I'd like to repeat: Service dogs are amazing. So amazing you can spot one from a mile away. They are highly trained, well behaved, and AWESOME. They obviously are allowed in the bar. NO PROBLEM.

Your dog is not a service animal. I know that, and so do you.

Did you know that the penalties for trying to pass a pet off as a service animal are getting steeper every day? Repeat after me: "FEDERAL FRAUD CHARGES."

Say that three times in a row. Then go ahead and sue.

You think that you have a highly trained, expensive service dog?

Wait until you meet my lawyer.

# 14

## Conclusion

So now we have reached the end.

I have enjoyed telling this story, and hopefully you have enjoyed reading it.

I love dive bars.

Maybe now you do too.

Please loan this book to anyone you know who is turning twenty-one, and we bartenders will be forever grateful to you in our hearts.

Thank you for reading.

Now go forth, minions! Enjoy your local tavern scene! Make the magic happen!

And tell your bartender I said hey.

Cheers!

Tanya

# Acknowledgments

I would like to thank my rad husband, Jason Frantzen; Mango "Gogo" Dummyhead Bulldog; and Dilly "Toofs" ButtButt Bulldog for being the best family a lady could ask for.

I'd also like to thank Joel, without whom I wouldn't have had the courage to open the B-Side; Patrick, for being the most amazing business partner; Diane, for designing, building, fixing, and maintaining my favorite places in the world; and Drew, Carisa, Vincent, Jake, Laura, Gabriel, Violet, Maureen, Jerry, Jerome, Jessica, Chanda, and Nina at B-Side Tavern and Dan, Nick, Britta, Jessi, Elise, Karen, and Roland at the Basement Pub for being the best coworkers and employees ever. Thank you all for your input and ideas regarding this book, and for everything I have learned and continue to learn from you about how to be an excellent bartender, employee, and boss.

Suzy, your friendship of a fellow female boss lady bar owner has saved my ass more times than I can count.

My friends and family, thank you for your love, patience, and support.

Thank you also to my coworkers and customers over the years and the amazing bar community of Portland.

While writing this book, I had a lot of help, which came in many forms—advice, inspiration, motivational support, art, music, delicious martinis, and feedback.

In addition to those mentioned above, I had very specific help from some people. Here they are: Violet Aveline for the amazing cover art and all the charming interior doodles and chapter headings; Matt Haley for the first cover and art, although I didn't end up using it my gratitude is no less; Jennifer Zaczek at Cypress Editing; Sarah Breeding and Dale Nibbe at Best Friends Publishing Services; and Kristina Rudinskas for marketing advice and support and years of friendship.

And you. Thank you for reading my silly little book.

Tanya Podolske Frantzen lives in Portland, Oregon, with her husband, Jason, and their two bulldogs. She currently owns and manages two neighborhood dive bars in Southeast Portland, the B-Side Tavern and the Basement Public House.

Made in the USA
San Bernardino, CA
28 July 2018